Book 20—Miracles

Healing
Minds and Bodies

Written by Anne de Graaf

Illustrated by José Pérez Montero

Family Time Bible Stories

Standard Publishing

Miracles – Healing Minds and Bodies

John 2—5; Luke 4—7, 11; Isaiah 53; Mark 1—3, 11; Matthew 5—10, 12

About Miracles—Healing Minds and Bodies

These stories are about the first years Jesus spends traveling and teaching. Thousands and thousands come to hear Him preach. Everyone from the most educated Pharisee to the poorest beggar wants to listen to Jesus.

What is it that draws so many to Him? Why does He become the talk of Jerusalem? Jesus offers something the people have not known for a long time. Jesus offers them God's love.

For hundreds of years the Jewish leaders have been turning the laws of Moses into a heavy burden for the people. They have added many small and difficult rules to the original laws God gave them. The educated Pharisees and Levites order the Jews to follow all these rules without teaching them the reasons why.

But God's laws are not just rules to follow so life will be hard. God's laws are there to help us live the best of all possible lives, healthy in mind and body, feeling loved and cared for by God.

The Jewish leaders do not like it when Jesus teaches about God's forgiveness and love. They know that Jesus' way means they will no longer be so important. So while many choose to believe Jesus and follow Him, there are others, mostly the religious leaders, who do not like Jesus. They become His enemies.

But friends and enemies alike are amazed as Jesus heals. The miracles Jesus performs are signs of God's love for His people. Healing minds and bodies is the Lord's way of showing His people that Jesus is the Son of God.

IN JERUSALEM
The Messy Temple

John 2:13-25

When Jesus and His followers arrived in Jerusalem, they went straight to the temple. Even as a boy, Jesus had called the temple "my Father's house."

But this time, instead of people praying to God and studying the laws of Moses, Jesus saw what looked more like a market than a temple.

There were people selling cows and birds. The temple rang with all the mooing and shouting. There were even people changing money. Jesus' disciples looked at Him. They could tell He was not pleased.

Suddenly, Jesus grabbed a whip. He

ran back and forth, driving the animals and people from the temple. "Get out!" He shouted. "Take these things away! Stop making my Father's house a marketplace!"

He turned over the tables of the money changers. Coins splashed all over the floor. Animals ran in every direction. People shouted, "Who is He? What gives Him the right?"

But Jesus' followers remembered how one of the prophets had said the Messiah would be very upset when He saw the people no longer treated God's house as a holy place.

During the next days of the feast, Jesus preached and did several miracles. Many people believed what He said.

The Man Who Dared Visit Only at Night

John 3:1-22

Most of the Jewish leaders did not like Jesus. They were jealous of how the people wanted to learn from Him. They saw Jesus as a threat because He claimed to be the Messiah and taught that salvation was for all people.

There were some religious leaders, though, who wondered at Jesus' wisdom. One was Nicodemus.

Nicodemus wanted to meet Jesus. But if the other Pharisees saw him speaking to Jesus, Nicodemus could get into a great deal of trouble. Late one night he snuck away to where he knew Jesus was staying. "God is with You," he said to Jesus.

Jesus greeted Nicodemus. He said, "If you are looking for the kingdom of God, then you need to know this. The only way for a man to see the kingdom of God is to be born again."

"But how can this be?" Nicodemus wondered.

Jesus said that anyone who wants to become His follower must become a new person, born of God's Holy Spirit. "I am not here to judge the world," Jesus said. "I am here to save the world. He who believes in God's Son is not judged, but he who does not believe has been judged already."

Nicodemus was amazed. He had never heard teaching like this.

JESUS IS LIVING WATER
He Is the Water of Life

John 4:1-26

As Jesus and His followers were traveling to Galilee, they passed through a land called Samaria.

No Jew ever wanted to talk to a Samaritan. But, when Jesus came to a well in Samaria, He sat down and started talking with a Samaritan woman there. "Give me a drink," He said.

She was surprised that a Jew would talk to her.

"Why do You, who are a Jew, talk to me, a Samaritan?" she asked.

Jesus said that if she knew who He was, she would be the one asking and He would have given her living water. This puzzled the Samaritan woman. Jesus said, "Whoever drinks of the water I give shall never be thirsty again."

"Oh, I want that!" the woman cried.

Then Jesus told her to get her husband. When she said she had no husband, Jesus told her all about her life, even how many husbands she had had. "And the man you are living with now is not your husband," He added.

The woman was amazed that He could know all her secrets. She tried to change the subject. When she asked about the Messiah, Jesus told her that He was the Savior!

The Woman at the Well

John 4:28-42

"Who is that woman at the well?" Jesus' disciples said to each other as they returned from the town where He had sent them to get food. They were surprised to see Him talking to a woman.

Jesus had given the woman a great deal to think about. She left her water pot behind and hurried back to town. "Come and see a man who told me all the things that I have done! Is it possible? Could this really be the Christ?"

The woman's story made the townspeople very curious. They followed her to the well and met Jesus. They listened to Him teach and felt their hearts and minds open to what He said. "Please, stay with us and tell us some more," they begged.

Jesus stayed in that town for two days and many people believed He was the Messiah. Some believed because of the story told by the woman at the well. But most believed Jesus himself. He taught about love and bothered to spend time with them, even though He was a Jew and they were Samaritans.

MAKING PEOPLE BETTER
Healing the Official's Son

John 4:46-54

Jesus returned to Cana in Galilee. A very important man came to see Him there. The man asked Jesus to come and heal his son, who was about to die.

Jesus said, "You people only believe when you see signs and wonders."

The man said again, "Please, Sir, come before my child dies."

Jesus said, "Go your way; your son lives."

The man looked at Jesus. "I believe Him," he thought. He turned and headed back home.

A day later, when the man was still walking home, one of his servants came running up to him. "Sir, your son is alive and well!" The man asked the servant when the boy got better. "Yesterday," the servant said. He named the exact time of day when Jesus had said, "Your son lives."

"This is the Messiah, then," the man thought. He and all his family believed.

There's No Place Like Home

Isaiah 53:3; Luke 4:14-30; John 4:44, 45

Jesus traveled from place to place, teaching all who came to hear Him. Eventually He came to Nazareth, the little town where He had grown up.

All the people were glad to see Him. They had heard how He could heal sick people, and they wanted to see for themselves if all the stories were true. But Jesus knew what the prophet Isaiah had taught many years earlier. Isaiah had said the Messiah would not be welcomed by His own people.

Jesus went to the synagogue in Nazareth, where the Jews worshiped God. He read from Isaiah's writings. "God has sent Me to free the prisoners and give sight to the blind." Then He said, "Today this Scripture has come true, even while you were listening."

All the people nodded their heads. "Doesn't Joseph's son read well?" they whispered to each other. But when they heard what Jesus said next, they grew angry.

"No prophet is welcome in his hometown. Even Elijah and Elisha healed only people who were not Jews." Jesus was saying that the gospel would be offered to any person with faith in Him, non-Jews as well as Jews.

The Jews grew so angry at this, they mobbed Jesus and tried to throw Him over a cliff. But He remained calm and simply walked away from them, even as they screamed for His death.

9

JESUS HEALS PEOPLE

Jesus Casts Out Demons

Mark 1:23-28; Luke 4:33-37

One day Jesus was in the synagogue in Capernaum. As He taught, all the men who knew the Jewish laws were amazed. "He talks as if He has spent His whole life studying," they said to each other.

Just then there was a man in the synagogue who was controlled by an unclean spirit. This man cried out, "What do we have to do with You, Jesus of Nazareth? Have You come to destroy us? I know who You are, the Holy One of God!"

The evil spirit knew well that Jesus was the Son of God. After all, Satan had tried to tempt Jesus in the desert for forty days. But Jesus did not want the people to be told who He was. Not yet. He wanted them to listen and choose for themselves.

Jesus said, "Be quiet, and come out of him!"

The unclean spirit cried out and threw the man it lived in onto the floor.

Then the spirit came out of him.

All the people watching were amazed. "Surely, He must be from God," they whispered to each other. "What is this? A new teaching with power! He commands even the unclean spirits, and they obey Him." The people were filled with wonder.

Peter's Mother-in-Law Is Healed

Matthew 8:14-17; Mark 1:29-39; Luke 4:38-44

After Jesus healed the man with the unclean spirit, news of what He had done spread far and wide. Peter and Andrew, James and John, and Jesus went to Peter's house.

Peter's mother-in-law was sick, with a fever. Jesus entered the woman's room and took her hand in His. He helped her stand up. Instantly, the fever left her. "I will get You something to eat, Teacher," she said, and fixed dinner for them all.

After the group had eaten, they opened the door and there was the whole town, waiting to see Jesus. Jesus healed many who were ill with different sicknesses. He cast out many demons and did not let them speak about who He was.

Finally, the people were gone. While His friends slept, Jesus got up and left the house. It was very early in the morning, and still quite dark. Jesus went out to a lonely place and prayed. When Jesus prayed, He was talking to His Father, who made Him strong and helped Him know what He should do next.

Peter and Andrew and James and John woke up and started searching for Jesus. When they found Him, they said, "Oh, Teacher! Everyone is looking for You."

But Jesus said that it was time to go to other towns to preach. "That is why I came," He said.

Jesus Heals a Leper

Matthew 8:1-4; Mark 1:40-45; Luke 5:12-16

As Jesus preached in Galilee, a leper came up to Him one day. Lepers are people with a terrible skin disease. It makes the people look very ugly on the outside.

Most forms of leprosy cannot be passed from one person to another. But in Jesus' day the people did not know that. They were very afraid of lepers and forced them to live outside the city. Lepers had no homes but the caves and no way to stay alive except to beg. Nobody dared touch a leper.

But Jesus was not afraid of the leper who came to Him. The leper fell to his knees in front of Jesus and said, "If You are willing, You can make me clean."

A look of understanding passed over Jesus' face. Here was a man who had no reason to hope, and yet he believed in Jesus. Jesus stretched out His hand and touched the leper. Jesus said, "I am willing; be cleansed."

Immediately, the leprosy left the man and his skin grew back normal. He stood up and looked at his healthy hands, tears streaming down his face. Jesus warned him not to say anything, but go and show the priest so he could be declared healthy and allowed back into the city.

But the leper was so excited, he ran and told everyone he met, "Jesus made me all better. Look! I am not a leper anymore!"

Four Men on the Roof

Matthew 9:2-8; Mark 2:1-12; Luke 5:18-26

There were people everywhere, crowded around the tiny house where Jesus was preaching. Four men carrying a stretcher made their way through the crowd. When they saw they could not even get to the door, they hauled the stretcher onto the roof.

On the stretcher lay a man who was paralyzed. His friends had brought him to see Jesus. They knew Jesus could make him better.

The four men began pulling tiles off the roof. They were making a hole! Inside the house, the people listening to Jesus looked up. The stretcher was being lowered through the hole!

Jesus saw how much faith the man's friends had and how hard they had worked to get him to Jesus so he would be healed. Jesus said to the man, "My son, your sins are forgiven." Jesus was telling him that all the wrong things he might have done in his life no longer mattered. He could start over.

But there were some Jewish scribes in the crowd who did not like Jesus. They said to themselves, "Who does He think He is? Only God can forgive sins!"

Jesus knew what they were thinking, though, and surprised them by answering, "Which is easier, to say 'Your sins are forgiven,' or to say, 'Get up and walk?' But just so you may know that the Son of Man has God's permission to forgive sins on earth, I say to you," he said to the paralyzed man, "get up and walk home."

The man did as he was told, just as if he had never been sick.

"Glory to God!" the people said. "We have seen wonderful things today!"

WHOM DID JESUS COME TO HELP?

The Tax Collector Says Yes

Matthew 9:9-13; Mark 2:14-17; Luke 5:27-32

The Jewish people did not like tax collectors. Even though tax collectors were also Jews, they worked for the Romans, who ruled over Israel during Jesus' time. Tax collectors often took more money from the people than they were supposed to.

Jesus saw a tax collector called Matthew. He said, "Follow me!"

Matthew had already heard much about Jesus. He jumped up from his table, leaving behind his record books and box of money, and followed Him.

A few evenings later, Jesus was sitting in Matthew's house, eating dinner. The people sitting with Him were all people the Jewish leaders thought of as bad. There were more tax collectors, and other sinners.

When the Jewish leaders, saw this, they asked, "Why does Jesus eat with these kind of people?"

But Jesus said, "Do the healthy need a doctor? No, the sick are the ones who need help. I have come to call sinners, not the righteous."

(Later, after Jesus' time on earth was over, Matthew wrote the part of the Bible that we call "The Gospel of Matthew.)

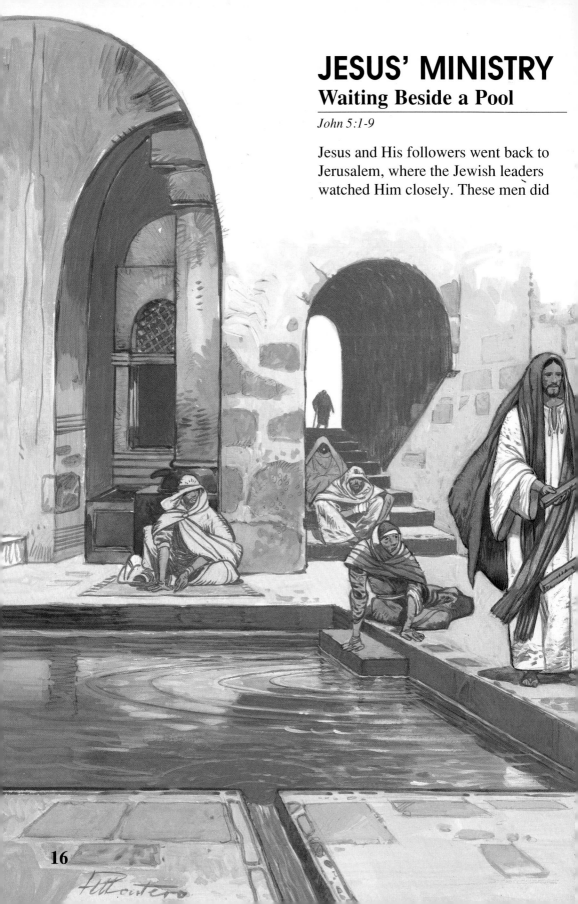

JESUS' MINISTRY
Waiting Beside a Pool
John 5:1-9

Jesus and His followers went back to
Jerusalem, where the Jewish leaders
watched Him closely. These men did

not like Jesus. "Jesus is too popular," they said to each other.

They did not like what He taught about the love of God being a gift for all people, not just the Jews. "We are the chosen people, after all," they said to each other. So they decided to try and trap Jesus.

There was a special gate in Jerusalem called Bethesda. Near that gate was a pool, with large steps. Many people lay on these steps, waiting for the water in the pool to move. They believed that in certain seasons an angel of God came and stirred the water. Whoever was the first one into the water after the angel came would get better.

When Jesus passed by the pool, He saw one man who had been trying for thirty-eight years to be the first one into the water.

Jesus knew the man had been sitting by the pool a long time. He said, "Do you want to get better?"

The sick man answered, "Sir, I have no one to put me into the pool when the water is stirred up."

Jesus said, "Get up. Pick up your bed and walk."

Immediately, the man was better, and he picked up his mat and began to walk!

Not on the Sabbath

Matthew 12:1-7; Mark 2:23-28; Luke 6:1-5; John 5:10-17

When the Jewish leaders saw the man carrying his mat, they said to him, "Don't you know no one may work on the Sabbath? Why are you carrying your bed? That is work."

The man said, "But the one who made me well said I should pick up my bed and walk."

"Who was that?" they asked him. He shrugged his shoulders. "I don't know."

Jesus had slipped away through the crowd.

Later, Jesus found the man in the temple and talked with him.

But once the man learned Jesus' name, he told the Jewish leaders, "Jesus was the one who healed me!"

On another Sabbath, Jesus and His disciples were passing through some grainfields. They were hungry, so they picked and ate the little pieces of wheat. The Pharisees said that was against the law on the Sabbath.

Jesus reminded them of King David and his men. They had been so hungry on a Sabbath that they went into the sacred tabernacle and ate bread that no one was allowed to eat.

Jesus was trying to show them that the day of rest was supposed to help people have healthy minds and bodies. If not working on the Sabbath hurt people, instead of helping them, that was not what God wanted.

Healing the Shriveled Hand

Matthew 12:8-14; Mark 3:1-6; Luke 6:6-11

Jesus went into the synagogue. As He passed by a man with a shriveled hand, the Pharisees pointed at the man. They asked Jesus, "What do You think? Is it allowed to heal on the Sabbath?"

Jesus had just finished telling them the Sabbath was for the good of the people. He turned to them with a stern face. "If you had one sheep and it fell into a hole on the Sabbath, would you save it? Isn't a man worth much more than a sheep? So yes! Of course it is allowed to heal on the Sabbath!"

All this was said while the man with the shriveled hand had been listening. Now Jesus said to the man, "Stretch out your hand!" The man did so, and his hand was completely healthy! He was so happy! Now he would not have to beg for a living. He could work hard and lead a normal life.

The Pharisees, though, were not so happy. They went outside and began to talk about how they could kill Jesus.

The Knowledge of God

John 5:18-47

The more Jesus preached and taught, the angrier the Pharisees became.

They did not like how popular Jesus was. They did not like His teaching that the love of God was for Jew and non-Jew. They did not like it when He called God His own Father, because that made Him equal with God.

The truth, of course, was that Jesus is God's Son. That is how He knew so much. That is why He could tell people their sins were forgiven. Jesus said He had the right to judge everyone, even those who were already dead.

Jesus reminded the Jewish leaders of the word God spoke when John the Baptist baptized Him. God had said, "You are My Son. I have always loved You. You have always pleased Me."

Jesus repeated what John had said, "This is the Lamb of God." For more proof, the people only had to see the miracles Jesus had done.

And Jesus was living exactly as the prophets had said the Messiah would live. Jesus was the Messiah the prophets had written about so many years earlier. He really was the Son of

God! Now it was up to the Pharisees to make the choice of believing...or not believing.

Many Are Healed Near Galilee

Matthew 12:15; Mark 3:7-12

When the Pharisees decided they would find a way to kill Jesus, Jesus left the area and went to the Sea of Galilee. A huge crowd of people followed Him, and He healed all who were sick.

Some of the people had unclean spirits in them. Whenever Jesus came near any of these people, the unclean spirits would cry out, "You are the Son of God!" But Jesus told them to be quiet because it was not time yet for the people to know who He was.

So many people wanted just to touch Jesus that He had to get into a nearby boat, to keep from being crushed.

Can you imagine what it would be like, to be sick all your life and then suddenly be well? That's what it was like to be near Jesus at this time.

The Twelve Apostles Are Set Apart

Matthew 10:1-23; Mark 3:13-19; Luke 6:12-16

After healing all the people in the crowd, Jesus went off by himself. He climbed up a mountain and prayed. All night long He prayed to God. And when the sun rose, He called His disciples to Him and chose twelve. These men would be His apostles. The twelve apostles would get to know the Son of God better than anyone else.

It was a strange group Jesus chose. Peter, Andrew, James, and John were fishermen. Matthew was a tax collector. Simon was mostly interested in fighting a war with the Romans to throw them out of Israel. The other men were Philip, Bartholomew, Thomas, another James, Judas Iscariot, and Thaddaeus.

After choosing the twelve, Jesus gave them special instructions. For the very first time, He would send others out to heal, in His name. These men were to go and do miracles, just as Jesus had.

"Go to the Jews and heal the sick, raise the dead, cleanse the lepers, cast out demons. Give freely," Jesus taught them. "Do not try to become rich. Trust in God's care, and you will have enough to eat. But things will not always be easy."

Jesus told them that some people would not welcome them or listen to their message.

Jesus was getting the apostles ready for the job they would do later. These were the men who would spread God's good news.

THE SERMON ON THE MOUNT
True Happiness

Matthew 5:1-12; Luke 6:20-49

Many, many people followed Jesus to a hillside. The teaching Jesus gave there is called the Sermon on the Mount.

On that hillside, Jesus taught the people about true happiness. To do as Jesus taught would give the people the best life possible.

As Jesus spoke, though, the people noticed He turned everything upside down. Instead of saying that the tough and pushy people would be successful, He said that meek people and those who depend on God are truly happy. This was something the people had never heard before.

"The most precious people in God's eyes are the poor, the hurting, and the gentle," Jesus said, "those who want very badly to see the right thing done. Those who have mercy and take care of others are very special. God richly blesses the peacemakers, as well as those who are hurt by others for doing what is right.

"If anyone hurts you because you believe in Me, be glad because you will be rewarded in Heaven. Remember, even the prophets were hurt by men when they spoke out for God."

Do You Know How to Be Salt?

Matthew 5:13-37

The people who, sat on the hillside, listening to Jesus' Sermon on the Mount, were astonished at His words. It was like no teaching they had ever heard before.

"You are the salt of the earth," Jesus said.

"But how can we be salt?" they asked.

The answer is that salt helps keep meat from spoiling, and makes food taste extra good. People who love God and live for Him keep our world from being entirely spoiled by sin. They change the "taste" of the world from sour to sweet.

"You are the light of the world. You cannot hide a city on a hillside," Jesus said, knowing the lights of a city would always give it away.

"No one hides a light under a basket," Jesus said. So people who follow God should let others see the way they live. Every man, woman, and child who loves God can show others a little of what God is like.

Jesus taught the people to think about the reasons for God's laws, and to always ask, "What is best for the people around me? How can I show them God's love?"

An Eye for an Eye

Matthew 5:38-48

There is a Jewish teaching, "An eye for an eye and a tooth for a tooth." In other words, if someone hurts you, his punishment is to have done to him whatever he did to you.

That was a rule by which the Jews had lived for hundreds of years. But Jesus turned that rule upside down.

He said to the people listening on the hillside, "If someone insults you with a slap on the right cheek, don't try to get even. Be willing to let him slap your other cheek, too."

"What's this?" the people gasped.

"And if anyone wants to sue you and take your shirt, let him have your coat as well," Jesus said.

Most people love their friends and hate their enemies. But Jesus said, "Love your enemies and pray for those who hurt you."

"But why, Lord? Why should we love and pray for people who hurt us?" the disciples asked Him. They were shaking their heads. They could not believe what Jesus was teaching.

Jesus answered, "Because your Father who is in Heaven wants you to be perfect. He lets the sun shine on good people, as well as bad. He sends the rain on kind and unkind people. It's not very hard for you to love your friends. But I want you to love friends and enemies, just as God loves everyone."

Talking to God

Matthew 6:1-15; 7:7-11; Mark 11:22-26; Luke 11:1-13

Jesus taught His followers to care for others, by giving to the poor and helping those who need it. "But beware of doing your good deeds when other people are watching," Jesus said. He wanted people to learn to love for the sake of loving, not for the sake of getting attention.

"When you give away your money, do it secretly. And your Father who sees in secret will pay you back.

"When you pray, do not show off to others. Go into a private place and when you have shut the door, pray to your Father in secret and your Father who sees in secret will pay you back."

"Teach us to pray," Jesus' followers said.

Jesus told them not to say the same prayer over and over again. They should talk to God like a Father. Then Jesus prayed out loud so the people could learn from Him.

"Father God who lives in Heaven, Your name is so holy. Let Your kingdom come. I pray everything on earth and in Heaven would be the way You want it. Please give us enough to eat today and forgive us for the things we have done wrong, in the same way that we have forgiven others. Help us to be strong and to do what is right. For the kingdom is yours, and power and glory are yours forever and ever. Amen."

Jesus said we should never give up praying. He said God will always hear our prayers. Sometimes God answers "yes," sometimes "no," and sometimes "wait." His answer is always what is best for us.

The Treasure Hunt

Matthew 6:19-34; Luke 12:22-32

During the Sermon on the Mount Jesus taught His followers how to search for hidden treasure. "Where your treasure is, that is where your heart will be," He said. What did He mean?

Treasures on earth can all disappear. The place to look for hidden treasure is in Heaven. "You cannot love money and love God," Jesus said. Which comes first?

Those who choose to follow God have nothing to worry about. "Don't worry about having enough to eat or drink, or how you will buy new clothes," Jesus taught.

"Look at the birds," He said, pointing at a flock flying overhead. "Your heavenly Father feeds them. And aren't you worth much more than

a bird? Why worry about clothes, then? God made flowers that are more beautiful than even the gowns of King Solomon."

God knows what people need. The most important thing is to follow Him, to obey Him. to love others as He does. God takes care of the rest.

How to Build a House

Matthew 7:24-29

As Jesus finished the Sermon on the Mount, He said, "Those of you who hear my words and do what I say are like the wise man who built his house on stone."

What happens to a house built on stone? It stays put, no matter if it rains hard or the winds blow.

"But," said Jesus, everyone who hears my words and does not do what I say will be like a foolish man who built his house on sand."

What happens to a house built on sand? As soon as a storm hits, as soon as floods rage, the house is swept away. "And you can be sure it falls hard," Jesus said.

As the people stood up and got ready to go home, they were all talking about what they had heard Jesus say.

"I've never heard anyone talk like Him before!"

"He must be the Son of God, He is so wise."

"No, I don't think so."

"Yes, I believe Him. I will become a follower of Jesus.

One thing they all agreed on. Everyone who heard Jesus preach that day was astounded at how sure He was of what He taught.

ASK AND YOU SHALL RECEIVE
The Faith of an Officer

Matthew 8:5-13; Luke 7:1-10

After the Sermon on the Mount, Jesus went to Capernaum. A Roman army officer was in charge of that town. He was a good and fair man who treated the Jews like a special people. He had even built a synagogue for the Jews in Capernaum.

This officer, who was called a centurion, had a sick slave. He cared for the slave very much and wanted him to get better. The centurion asked some Jewish leaders to ask Jesus if He would come and heal the slave.

Jesus was close to the officer's house when the centurion sent friends to tell Him, "The centurion says, 'Lord, do not trouble yourself further. I am not a good enough man for You to come under my roof. I am not even worthy to come to You. But just say the word and I know my servant will be healed.'

Jesus turned to the crowd that followed Him. "Do you hear this?" He called out. "I have not found this kind of faith in any of the Jews."

Jesus had come to be the Messiah of the Jewish people. Yet few had believed Him. The centurion was not even a Jew, but he knew who Jesus was. He knew the Son of God could heal his slave by just saying so.

And it happened just that way. When the friends returned to the centurion's house, they found the slave was well.

The Boy Who Came Back to Life

Luke 7:11-16

People who followed Jesus from town to town had seen Him heal the sick, make the blind see and the crippled walk. There were still those, though, who did not believe Jesus was the Messiah. "Perhaps He is a great and wise doctor, but nothing more," they said.

When Jesus went to the town of Nain, these doubters had to think again.

As He entered the town, followed by the usual crowd, a funeral passed by Him. A woman was crying for her dead son, who was to be buried. She was very, very sad because her son had been her only family.

When Jesus saw the woman, He hurt with her. "Do not cry," He said. He came up and touched the coffin. "Young man!" He said, "I say to you, get up!"

And the dead man sat up and began talking! Jesus gave him back to his mother.

The people were filled with wonder. "Only God has power over life and death. Surely this is God visiting His people."

The story of the widow's son who came back to life in Nain spread far and wide. When people heard it, many believed in Jesus as God's Son.

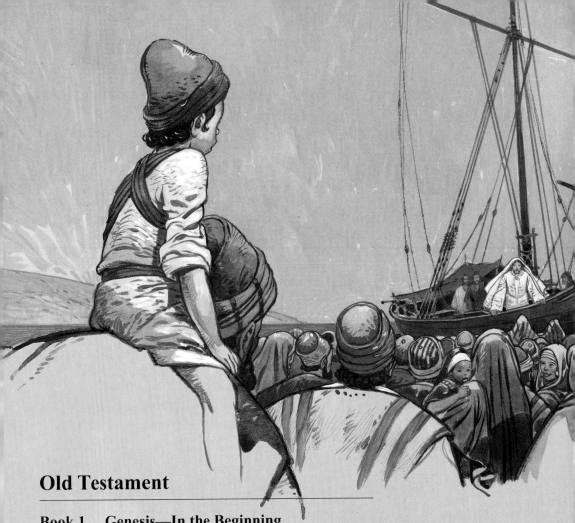

Old Testament

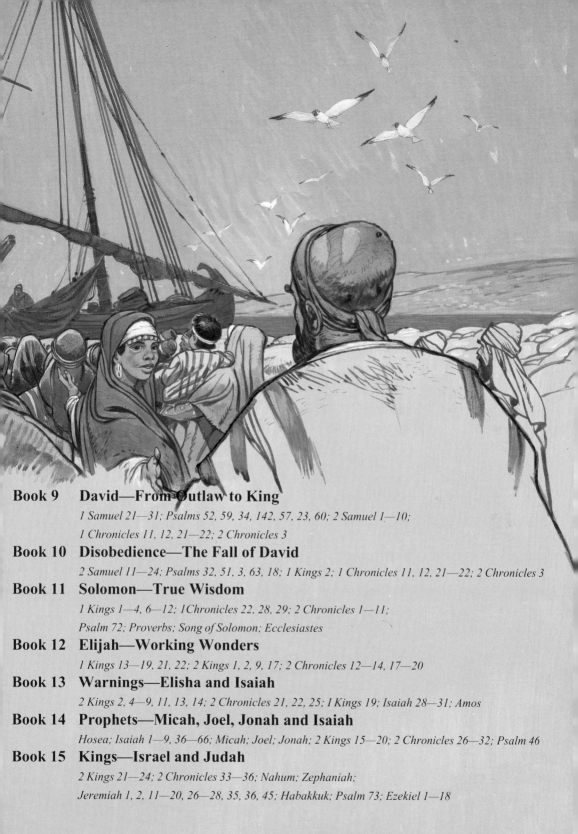

New Testament